I0419837

Grow Fruit Indoors

Easily And Frugally Grow Fruit Indoors With Plants And Fruit Trees And Enjoy Organic Exotic Fruits In Weeks!

David Wright

Copyright © 2015 David Wright

STOP!!! Before you read any further....Would you like to know the secrets of Anti-Aging?

If your answer is yes, then you are not alone. Thousands of people are looking for the secret to reducing wrinkles, looking younger, and maintaining a youthful appearance.

If you have been searching for these answers without much luck, you are in the right place!

Not only will you gain incredible insight in this book, but because I want to make sure to give you as much value as possible, right now for a limited time you can get full **100% FREE access to a VIP bonus EBook** entitled **Anti-Aging Made Easy!**

Just Go Here For Free Instant Access:

www.LuxyLifeNaturals.com

Legal Notice

All rights reserved. Without limiting the rights under the copyright reserved above, no part of this publication may be reproduced, stored in or introduced into a retrieval system, or transmitted, in any form, or by any means (electronic, mechanical, photocopying, recording, or otherwise) without the prior written permission of the copyright owner and publisher of this book. This book is copyright protected. This is for your personal use only. You cannot amend, distribute, sell, use, quote or paraphrase any part or the content within this eBook without the consent of the author or copyright owner. Legal action will be pursued if this is breached.

Disclaimer Notice

Please note the information contained within this document is for educational and entertainment purposes only. Considerable energy and every attempt has been made to provide the most up to date, accurate, relative, reliable, and complete information, but the reader is strongly encouraged to seek professional advice prior to using any of this information contained in this book. The reader understands they are reading and using this information contained herein at their own risk, and in no way will the author, publisher, or any affiliates be held responsible for any damages whatsoever. No warranties of any kind are expressed or implied. Readers acknowledge that the author is not engaging in the rendering of legal, financial, medical, or any other professional advice. By reading this document, the reader agrees that under no circumstances is the author, publisher, or anyone else affiliated with the production, distribution, sale, or any other element of this book responsible for any losses, direct or indirect, which are incurred as a result of the use of information contained within this document, including, but not limited to, -errors, omissions, or inaccuracies. Because of the rate with which conditions change, the author and publisher reserve the right to alter and update the information contained herein on the new conditions whenever they see applicable.

Table Of Contents

Introduction

I want to thank you and congratulate you for purchasing the book, *Grow Fruit Indoors: Easily And Frugally Grow Fruit Indoors With Plants And Fruit Trees And Enjoy Organic Exotic Fruits In Weeks!*

This "Grow Fruit Indoors" book contains proven steps and strategies on how you can start growing delicious fruits indoors within a short span of time. Inside, you'll find different information that will not only encourage you to take part in this worthwhile hobby but also provide the knowledge needed to get started with it.

Here's what you'll find within the chapters of this book:

1. Grow Fruit Indoors and Its Benefits
2. Getting Started with Indoor Gardening
3. Pros and Cons of Backyard Gardening
4. Preppers Survival Pantry
5. Seed Saving
6. Mini Farming
7. Fruit Infused Water
8. Square Foot Gardening
9. Frugally Grow Fruit Indoors with Plants and Fruit Trees
10. Enjoy Organic Exotic Fruits in Weeks

We hope that you find all that you need to get started in this book and that it becomes one of the best guides for you when it comes to indoor fruit gardening.

Thanks again for purchasing this book, I hope you enjoy it!

Chapter 1: Grow Fruit Indoors And Its Benefits

One of the most common questions that people ask about growing their own food indoors would be the benefits that may come from it. How is it different from simply buying fruits from the grocery, which is much less difficult and barely involves any work? It is the idea of gardening that turns many people off away from the hobby itself, thinking that it would be too hard and not worth it. This is, of course, false. Getting started requires minimal effort and the benefits are bountiful. To help you better understand, here are some of the top benefits that come with growing your own fruit at home.

- Get the right kind of nutrition and enjoy much tastier fruits. Research has shown that organically grown foods actually contain far more vitamins, minerals and nutrients than the ones grown using synthetic fertilizers and pesticides. There is a good reason as to why chefs would much rather use fresh and organic ingredients; not only do they taste better, they are also much healthier. By growing your own fruits, you know exactly what goes into the soil that nourishes the plant so you also don't have to worry about getting sick from it.

- Lower your food budget and save more money for other necessities. Growing your fruits means that you don't have to spend money on buying some from the grocery which can be quite expensive-- especially if you're keen on trying out exotic, tropical fruits. Surveys have shown that people can end up spending hundreds of dollars every month on store bought fruits that don't nourish them as much as home-grown organically farmed ones. So weigh the pros and cons; certainly, you'll see which one is more worth it.

- Help prevent soil erosion. Did you know that the Soil Conservation Service in the United States actually estimates that at least 3 billion tons of topsoil are eroded every year? This means that it erodes much faster than the natural build up and if it continues at this rate, the people may not even have enough soil to plant their crops in. In the food chain, soil is at the very foundation. Therefore, in farming your fruit indoors and organically, you will be helping in the prevention of topsoil erosion.

— The greener alternative. Sticking to the theme of helping the environment, it is no secret that planting your own food also helps the environment. To begin with, you're producing much less carbon dioxide since you're not using machinery like the one used in larger farms. You are also using organic pesticides so you're able to keep the quality and overall health of the soil you've planted in. Note that synthetic fertilizers and pesticides, in the long run, can actually do more damage to the soil than good.

— Reduce the carcinogens around you by a significant amount. The EPA or Environment Protection Agency actually estimates that pesticides, ones that are known as carcinogens, increase the risk of people contracting the disease simply by consuming mass farmed fruits and vegetables. At the same time, it also pollutes the groundwater, which is the primary source of potable water for more than half of the entire country's population. Would you really want this to continue happening?

— Build an extra source of income for yourself. Besides being able to help the environment and making sure that you only eat the healthiest and freshest produce, did you know that this could also become an extra source of income for yourself? Well, if you happen to get a bountiful harvest, you can opt to sell the produce at a farmer's market and get back some of the money you invested into building the garden itself. Continue doing this and not only will you have a sustainable source of food but you'll also have one that pays for itself-- in cash.

Chapter 2: Getting Started With Indoor Gardening

So, you're up for the challenge of growing your own fruits indoors? Well, to help you get started, here are a few of the things that you need to consider.

- Space. Your indoor garden can take up as big or as a little a space as you're willing to give it. You can grow any kind of crops without needing such a huge space. In fact, a balcony garden can produce enough fruit for two people. You will need to invest in good quality plant growers and the size depends on the need of the plant you've chosen so make sure you pick the ones that suit the space you have available. If you're handy with carpentry, installing planting/grower shelves is also a good idea for creating more area and space for your plants.

- Light. Plants need light in order to photosynthesize; this is just their basic need in order to survive. Providing your plants with adequate lighting will allow them to grow better and produce more. However, you must also consider the amount of light that a particular crop needs. For this, check the information on the seed packet itself. It should tell you the exact amount of light and water needed by the plant itself. Make sure that you have enough well-sunned areas in your home so that you don't compact your crops too much as that might hinder their growth.

- Selecting grow lights. In case natural light isn't readily available, as is the case with most apartment gardens, you may choose to go with a grow light. There are many different types available and they are sure to suit your needs. The most efficient kind for indoor gardening would be the HID or High Intensity Discharge bulbs. However, they can also be pretty expensive so do look into finding more affordable versions of it.

- Temperature. This can be quite tricky especially for beginners but it is also very important. To begin with, you have to choose plants that thrive within a certain range so that you do not need to make too many adjustments. Typically, 65-75° F would be the best for many plants. However, if you're unsure, check the packet again for some information or ask your local grower when you go and buy your seeds.

–   Humidity. Again, another tricky thing to try and keep a proper balance of when it comes to gardening indoors. Humidity changes along with the seasons so you need to be aware of this. Luckily, there are also simple things that you can do to maintain it during the drier months. Simple misting every single day is already helpful in preventing your plants from shrivelling up. You can also place a tray of water near your garden; this would add moisture to the air through evaporation. Even running a humidifier would help. This can benefit your skin as well.

–   Choosing a growing medium. Your growing medium will serve as the foundation for your garden so you need to choose the right one. Never opt to simply get soil from the outside because for your seedlings, it is inappropriate. It would be too heavy and may contain pests as well as weeds that are both instant crop killers. The soft roots of the seedlings would only thrive in loose growing mix, one that is loose and would drain well but is capable of holding just the right amount of moisture, and nutrients for your growing crops. You can ask your local plant needs store for the best brand they carry.

–   Watering. Since you're growing indoors, one thing you need to keep in mind is that plants that are grown in containers do have a tendency to dry out quicker than their outside-grown counterparts. This is why they need frequent watering. When doing so, it would be best to use room-temperature water and make sure that you pour enough that it begins to drip from the drain holes of your container or plant pot. If the container comes with a saucer, remove this as it can actually cause root rot (from the collected water).

- Fertilizer. Plants that are grown indoors would need an extra boost when it comes to nutrients so fertilizers are certainly important. While the growing medium you'll buy would have some of what they need, this would quickly diminish as the plants grow. For organic farming, make sure that you only use natural fertilizers-- composting would be key for this.

Chapter 3: Pros And Cons Of Backyard Gardening

At some point during your indoor gardening venture, you might consider backyard gardening (if you have the space) as an extension of your current project. This is not a bad idea, of course, and many people are doing the same thing. Making use of the spaces they have available for more than just storing and keeping things. A small area can be turned into an efficient garden once you have everything you need to set it up. Is this a sustainable way to produce food for yourself and your family? Yes.

So, to help you understand backyard gardening more, here are some pros and cons that you might want to consider before getting started.

- Ecological impact: pro. Homegrown fruits (or any other produce) require much less energy when it comes to producing, packaging and transporting. This is one of the main reasons as to why green activists prefer it over buying from supermarkets. It is more sustainable too in terms of making sure the environment is not harmed during the process of farming. Of course, one must also consider that growing fruits at home also makes use of much less pesticides and artificial fertilizers (if any at all) and leans towards more healthier, greener gardening practices.

- Health benefits: pro. First off, you'll get a significant amount of exercise while tending to your garden. Whether it be a backyard one or something indoors, you will still exert a certain amount of physical labor, which can help you burn calories, improve muscle function and strength. It is also a known fact that people who grow their own foods are also more likely to eat the freshest produce, which are high in fiber and very low in fat. In doing that, you are also preserving your overall health.

- Financial considerations. neutral. In theory, growing your own food would be a great way to save money. However, this is not always the case but only for first timers.

Equipment and the supplies you'll need to set everything up can be expensive. It might also take a while before you see any returns on these investments but once you get a good system going, it would start paying for itself. Even more so if you opt to sell some of the excess that you harvest.

- Potential crop loss: con. Home gardeners will often experience this, beginners most especially, because some insects simply cannot be eradicated with natural pesticides. Chemical pesticides do offer a solution but these can actually cause long-term health problems along with ecological damage. Note that you'll be doing this inside your home so it's best to simply stay away from these toxic substances.

- Time input: con. If you live a fast-paced, always on the go kind of life then you might have some trouble trying to fit in a home garden into your schedule. It would require a fairly significant investment when it comes to time; this is regardless of the technique you apply to it. Some gardeners can spend up to seven whole hours simply making sure that everything in their gardens are working well. It is a very rewarding hobby but do make sure you have enough time in a day to really tend to your garden's needs.

Chapter 4: Prepper's Survival Pantry

Building an emergency pantry, also known as a prepper's pantry, is considered by many as one of the lifelines that could very well mean the difference between perishing and survival in the event of an emergency. To some, the idea seems morbid and a grim look at how the future might be like-- but the simple point of the matter is that nobody knows what could happen in the future. Right now, being interested in growing your own food at home can be considered preparing for the future. In fact, it is one of the recommended projects for every prepper. A sustainable.

So, if you're interested in starting your own prepper's pantry, here are some of the things that you need to consider:

- Choose foods that don't require any form of refrigeration.
- Foods that don't require (or need very little of) fuel and electricity.
- Make sure that the items have a long shelf life.
- It should be able to provide you and your family with ample nutrition and must also contain a certain amount of salt.
- Water. For cooking and drinking purposes. So make sure you have a lot of this in stock and that the containers are sanitary. If you can have a sustainable source of potable water, this would be good as well.

The basic prepper's pantry should have the following:

- Canned fruits, vegetables, soups and meats. Sauces should be included in this category as well

- Dried legumes such as beans, peas and lentils

- Nuts and nut butters

- Pasta, flour (white or whole wheat), whole grains

- Seasonings, bouillon cubes and any kitchen staple that you often use

- Jell-o or different pudding mixes

- Honey, cocoa powder, dried milk

- Plant based oils

- Packaged meals (ramen included)

- Fruit juices, drink mixes, coffee and tea

- Seeds for eating and sprouting

*Keeping a seed bank is also very beneficial for your prepper's pantry. Choose the seeds well and make sure that they are suitable for growing indoors and will not require too much of your resources should you need to plant it during the time of emergency.

Chapter 5: Seed Saving

When it comes to seed saving/storing, there are a few important things that you must take note of in order to ensure that they are preserved well for future use. To help you understand this better, here are a few tips to keep in mind.

Seed Saving 101:

- Think cool and dry regardless of where you'll be storing your seeds. Humidity coupled with warmth can instantly shorten the shelf life for these seeds; it doesn't matter what kind they are.

- Storing them in the packets? Always make sure you keep the packet itself in food storage bags, mason jars with tight lids, plastic film canisters or glass canisters that come with gasket lids. This is to keep everything airtight.

- The fridge is one of the best storage areas for your seeds. However, do keep the seed containers away from the freezer section as this may produce moisture.

- Another great way to keep your seeds dry would be to add a milk packet to the storage container. To do this, just add powdered milk to 4 layers of fascial tissue, fold it up well then place it together with the seeds. An easier alternative to this would be using silica gel.

- Store each year's seeds in the same container and make sure that you add labels on it. Because most seeds can only last 3 years, you will want to know at a glance if a particular packet has past its "prime" when it comes to planting.

- Ready to plant? Remove your containers from the fridge (or wherever you stored them) and let these warm up to room temperature before opening. If not, you risk introducing moisture from the air to the seeds, which can cause them to start clumping together.

- If you gather seeds from your own plants, make sure you dry them first before packing. Spread them out on some tissue or newspaper for at least a week and do make sure that you add labels too, to avoid confusion. Once dried, pack them in small envelopes and again, label them with the specifics such as date and plant variety. Remember, if you're looking to save your own plant seeds then you will need to sow open-pollinated varieties as this would come back true whilst hybrids won't.

- Lastly, do come to terms with the fact that no matter how methodical you are when it comes to saving your seeds, there are instances wherein they simply won't germinate. This could be due to climate reasons or even unhealthy seeds overall. It doesn't mean that you did a step wrong, however. This is one of the reasons why you should be more prolific when saving and planting; in doing so, you increase your success rate significantly.

Chapter 6: Mini Farming

For urban dwellers, the idea of having their own "farm" or producing their own food seems a little farfetched given the small amount of space allotted to each person. However, mini farming provides a solution for that and turns a small backyard plot into a sustainable food resource.

Of course, before you get started, there are a few things you must consider. Here are a few tips that should help you begin off on the right foot.

- Location is key. Since you'll be working with a raised bed, having it face southwards would be one of the best positions you can put it in. Make sure that your tallest crops are always in the back. It would also be good if you're able to have it near a water source so that tending to it becomes just a bit more easier.

- Think of the sun. Keep in mind that your garden would need at least 6 hours of sunlight each day. Whether it be morning or afternoon sun, both would work. Determining the amount of sun you get each day, especially if you're not one to pay attention, can be a pretty daunting task. If you have time to spare during the weekend, try standing in different areas of your garden at different hours during the day. Snap a photo of the sunlight the spot gets and compare each by the end of the day.

- Remember the Goldilocks rule. This refers to the "not too much and not too little" philosophy that you need to apply when it comes to planting. You wouldn't want to plant so much that some of it ends up rotten because you weren't able to consume or give them all away. However, you shouldn't plant so little that you're not even able to make a meal out of it. So if you want to have peas, you need to have more than seven and so on. Also, plant the kind of produce that you do like to make sure that you'll actually end up eating them.

- Slopes and hills. A gentle slope or an even ground would be best for your raised bed. However, if it can't be helped and you need to work with a steeper hill than you have to terrace your raised beds into the slope itself. This should require a bit of expertise but if you'd rather work on it yourself, there are many guides available that would walk you through the process itself.

- Choose your crops well. Besides thinking of the amount, you also need to consider the kind of plants you'll be grouping together. Their height, needs and so on. More or less, they need to match each other to make planting and maintenance less complicated for you.

- Lastly, make sure that you prepare all the tools and equipment you'll be needing for your garden beforehand. This should help you avoid unnecessary hassles come planting time.

Chapter 7: Fruit Infused Water

If you're looking to cut down on your intake of fizzy drinks but don't like plain old water then here's a great alternative that you should try: Fruit Infused Water. Not only is it much healthier, it's also very easy to prepare and since you'll soon be planting your own fruits indoors you'll be able to enjoy it at its freshest.

The preparation for it is really easy and straight up, without needing any complicated tools or kitchen equipment. The best bit? Everyone in your family can enjoy and benefit from it. It isn't unusual for kids to opt for juices instead of drinking water but with this, they'll be able to properly hydrate themselves without you getting a headache from trying to get them to do it.

Fruit infused water can help you with more than just staying hydrated. It can also help in boosting your energy as well as detoxifying your insides, aiding your digestive system when it comes to functioning more efficiently.

How to:

- Simply slice up your fruits and peel them if needed.

- Once done, fill a pitcher with some water, add as much fruit as you'd like into it and allow to sit for at least 30 minutes so that the flavors would start to infuse.

- No need to add sugar!

- Chill before serving and that's it! Easy enough, right?

Some mixes that you might want to try:

- Green tea, lime and mint. This helps with quicker fat burning and metabolism, congestion, headaches and freshens your breath. Great as a side drink when you're having your lunch meals.

- Kiwi and strawberry. This helps in boosting your immune system protection, your cardiovascular health, digestion and blood sugar regulation.

- Lemon, cucumber and lime. This boosts your Vitamin C and strengthens your immune system defense. It also prevents heartburn but for that, do drink it at room temperature.

These are also great alternatives to your typical sports drink. Have them before and after you've worked out to help detoxify your body and boost your energy.

Chapter 8: Square Foot Gardening

Much like mini farming, square foot gardening is something that you can easily do right at home with not a lot of complications and harvest a good amount of produce that's typically enough to feed 2 people. Now, to help you get started right, here are some of the considerations that you need to keep in mind when it comes to square foot gardening.

–   Selecting where you'll place the square foot. Again, this is important because crops need enough sunlight in order to grow well. Fruits, for one, require direct sunlight everyday so choose an area that's away from any trees that you have in your yard.

–   Start with a small bed. 4 x 4 foot raised beds are the most manageable and having two of these should be enough to fit your crops if you choose them well. The useful thing about building a raised bed is that you need not do any additional soil work for it. The kits that you can buy online or in any gardening supplies store would provide you with all that you need to construct it. Some of them even come with self-watering varieties that effectively reduce the amount of work that you need to do in setting everything up. Do note, however, that these kits can be quite expensive.

–   Type of soil to use. There are many different varieties but only a specific few can work for what you need. Once you've picked out the fruits that you intend to plant, do some research on the kind of soil that they thrive in best. If you're using two beds then make sure that you group together, the crops that have the same (or at least similar) needs. This should help minimize any complications for you.

- Use compost! Keep a compost bin in your kitchen where you can place all of your compostable scraps. Using compost is the most environmentally friendly way of fertilizing your soil and the best thing about it is that it's absolutely free. You just have to be very diligent when it comes to putting it together. This is one way of recycling things that could still be used, making sure that nothing in your home goes to waste. Even fallen leaves can be added to the mix!

- Make sure you include a way of protecting your plants from harsh weather in your plans. Simple things like a screen should shield them from too much sun or even a makeshift "roof" for when the rain gets too strong. Simple but effective.

Chapter 9: Frugally Grow Fruit Indoors With Plants And Fruit Trees

Many people tend to think that growing fruit bearing plants indoors is impossible. However, this is certainly not the case. While a mango tree won't fit in your living room, there are other varieties that take up very little space and grow so abundantly, you'll be able to feed your family.

Here are a few examples:

- Strawberries. These are quite easy to grow and can be planted in flower pouches, hanging baskets or even a window box. You'll be able to harvest them come the summer and even turn some into jam which you can either sell or give as gifts.

- Raspberries. Autumn fruiting raspberries are good additions to your indoor garden. They are easy to grow and can be planted even in the smallest of spaces available. They are also very easy to maintain and are quite prolific so you'll get to enjoy them in a variety of different ways.

- Blueberries. A favorite dessert topper or just a snack, blueberries are very easy to grow and require very little in order to flourish. A window box or a hanging basket would work best for them, however. The only real downside to it is that it usually takes at least 3 years before it actually produces fruit. In the meantime, however, they do make an attractive indoor plant.

- Figs. Looking to add a Mediterranean flair to your indoor garden? Figs would do just that. These require lots of sunlight and can be grown in containers where their roots are restricted. In fact, they produce more in this state. Choose a window box for them, and place it against a sunny west or southern wall. They take a bit of time before they fruit but it is well worth the wait.

- Apples. Apple trees are a real asset for any size garden, especially if they produce prolifically. You can make pies with it, make jams, make applesauce and even wine! A dwarf family apple tree would be your best bet if you're growing indoors, however. Just make sure it gets lots of sun and that you tend to it regularly. All the work would be rewarded once it started fruiting.

Chapter 10: Enjoy Exotic Organic Fruits In Weeks!

When it comes to indoor fruit gardening, it isn't just the regular varieties that you can choose to plant. There are a number of different tropical and exotic fruit bearing plants that you can easily grow in your home. Most of these require very minimal maintenance, which means that you need not worry about adding more to what you have to do on a daily basis.

Interested? Well, here are some of the best examples that you can try:

–   Pineapple. Contrary to popular belief, pineapples can be easily grown indoors and this requires very minimal effort to do so. To get started, all you really need is the top of any store bought pineapple, plant this in a fairly large and deep container using regular potting mix. Tip: find a pineapple that has firm green leaves without any sign of wilting. These grow the best. The plant itself likes a lot of sun and must be kept moist. Once grown, it can reach up to 6 feet in height and almost just as wide.

–   Avocado. While you can grow an avocado plant from its seed, it typically grows slowly and would not be able to produce any fruit. What you need to do is purchase a plant from a nursery and transfer it into your home garden. This particular plant favors loose, sandy loam so do make sure you have that as well. Much like the pineapple, it requires a lot of sun as well as cool evening temperatures. Keep them moist but don't overwater as it doesn't like wet soil at all.

–   Guava. These are small trees that give off a very subtle scent so they're nice to have around the house as a natural air freshener as well. Guavas, if you're not too familiar with it, are green skinned fruits that are refreshing to eat or add into salads. As for the plant, it thrives well in rich dirt so make sure you add in a lot of organic matter. Dried leaves and grass trimmings are good for this purpose. You can use any kind of soil but do make sure its salt content isn't too high. They also need to be watered regularly.

- Pomegranates. These tend to be quite compact so they would thrive well in containers. They do need quite a lot of sun so anywhere that gets lot of sunlight would be a good spot to place them in. These bloom during springtime and produce lovely, blood orange flowers. However, if you want the plant to produce fruit, you'll need to purchase plants from a nursery and transfer it to your indoor garden.

Conclusion

Thank you again for purchasing the book *Grow Fruit Indoors: Easily And Frugally Grow Fruit Indoors With Plants And Fruit Trees And Enjoy Organic Exotic Fruits In Weeks!*

I am extremely excited to pass this information along to you, and I am so happy that you now have read and can hopefully implement these strategies going forward.

I hope this book was able to help you understand the different ways through which you can start planting crops at home as well as the things you need to know when it comes to planting different plants. The next step is to get started using this information and to hopefully live a much healthier and greener life!

Please don't be someone who just reads this information and doesn't apply it, the strategies in this book will only benefit you if you use them! If you know of anyone else that could benefit from the information presented here please inform them of this book.

Finally, if you enjoyed this book and feel it has added value to your life in any way, please take the time to share your thoughts and post a review on Amazon. It'd be greatly appreciated!

Thank you and good luck!

Preview Of:

The #1 Preppers Survival Guide!

<u>Preppers Survival Guide</u>

Stop Bugging Out! - Get Prepared With Fast & Easy Tips For Food Storage, Water Storage Canning, And Preserving!

Introduction

I want to thank you and congratulate you for purchasing the book, *"Preppers Survival Guide: Stop Bugging Out! - Get Prepared With Fast & Easy Tips For Food Storage, Water Storage Canning, And Preserving!"*

This "Preppers Survival Guide" book contains proven steps and strategies on how to successfully prepare for crisis, SHTF's (Shit-Hits-The-Fan) and other emergency situations. Through this book, you will be able to understand the vital principles to becoming an effective prepper.

Preparing for survival does not mean that you are looking forward to doomsday or to any major disasters. It simply means that you are concerned for your family's welfare and you want to make sure that your family has security and comfort during times of major crisis.

Thanks again for purchasing this book, I hope you enjoy it!

Chapter 1: The Preppers Survival Guide

You and your family's survival do not only pertain to prepping or to the comical antics done by TV survivalist. Each day, real people face life and death situations where they need to rely on their preparedness and their abilities to overcome a natural disaster or accident. You do not need to wait for an emergency situation to happen in your life because you decide to learn the following vital survival skills that can help you overcome any emergency situation:

1. First Aid. You need to realize that accidents can occur anywhere and any day. When you have solid first aid skills, you can help not only your own family but other people, as well, while waiting for the professional medics to arrive. You can opt to take classes or read books to learn how to provide emergency first aid care.

2. Building a Fire. Fires do not only provide warmth during cold weathers. They are also useful in keeping predators away, cooking food, and boiling water. Because of the modern amenities that you enjoy every day, you may have taken for granted this very skill. But learning how to build a fire can be a critical still for you to survive in the wilderness.

3. Putting Up a Shelter. You can keep yourself and your family dry and warm when you know how to put up a shelter. You need to learn how to use different materials such as grasses, branches of trees and other man-made material to create a comfortable shelter that can protect you from harsh natural elements.

4. Hunting, Trapping and Fishing. Obtaining food has become easy for all of us. Because of online stores, we do not even need to get out of our house to buy food. But during survival situations, your skills in hunting, building traps, setting snares and fishing using different methods can make sure that you and your family have enough food in order to stay alive.

5. Gardening and Foraging. Along with hunting, foraging is another vital skill that you need during survival situations. You can take classes, or read books to know more about the plants in

your local area that are safe to eat. But simple foraging may not be enough for long-term survival. You also need to learn how to plant your own garden to make sure that you and your family can have food in the long-term.

6. Physical Fitness. During survival situations, you always need to be alert and quick to respond. In order to do so, you need to make sure that your body is physically fit not only to work more efficiently during stressful situations but also to avoid getting sick or injured during emergencies.

7. Resourcefulness. It is ideal to start practicing how to make things using scraps and other materials that you have inside your house. Through constant practice, you will develop the skill in using simple things for various purposes.

8. Defense. During emergency situations, one of your primary objectives is to defend yourself, your family and your home. It is ideal for you to start going to different classes and learn home defense, martial arts, shooting or other defensive skills.

Thanks for Previewing My Exciting Book Entitled:

"Preppers Survival Guide: Stop Bugging Out! - Get Prepared With Fast & Easy Tips For Food Storage, Water Storage Canning, And Preserving!"

To purchase this book, simply go to the Amazon Kindle store and simply search:

"PREPPERS SURVIVAL GUIDE"

Then just scroll down until you see my book. You will know it is mine because you will see my name "David Wright" underneath the title.

Alternatively, you can visit my author page on Amazon to see this book and other work I have done. Thanks so much, and please don't forget your free bonuses

DON'T LEAVE YET! - CHECK OUT YOUR FREE BONUSES BELOW!

Free Bonus Offer: Get Free Access To The www.LuxyLifeNaturals.com VIP Newsletter!

Once you enter your email address you will immediately get free access to this awesome newsletter!

But wait, right now if you join now for free you will also get free access to the "Secrets of Becoming A Meditation Expert – In 7 Days!" free Ebook!

To claim both your FREE VIP NEWSLETTER MEMBERSHIP and your FREE BONUS Ebook on the SECRETS OF BECOMING A MEDITATION EXPERT IN 7 DAYS!

Just Go To:

www.LuxyLifeNaturals.com

www.ingramcontent.com/pod-product-compliance
Lightning Source LLC
Chambersburg PA
CBHW061940280526
45787CB00004B/1665